READY...SET...PREPARE!

A DISASTER PREPAREDNESS ACTIVITY BOOK

Special Note to Parents and Guardians, Teachers, and Leaders

Remember to learn about the emergency plans that are in place at your child's school, child care facility, or other places where your child stays when not with you. Contact the school principal's office, child care facility, or responsible adult to find out how evacuations and other emergency procedures will be handled while your child is in their care. Also, make sure to **always** keep up-to-date emergency contact information on file at the school or with the adult caring for your child.

Hey Everybody!

We are the Disaster Crew! We are here to help you learn how to prepare for disasters. I am Snowy Singh, and if you are like me, you have heard reports about all sorts of disasters on the TV news and in newspapers. The fact is that disasters can happen anywhere at any time. And that can be a scary thought. But here is another fact: The better prepared you are, the safer you will be!

That's why the entire Disaster Crew – Stormy Knight, Blaze Martinez, Tommy Twister, Johnny Hurricane, Rising Waters, "Quake" Johnson, and me – has pitched in to help teach you the best ways to get ready for a disaster!

Each topic in this book has a fun game created just for you by the Disaster Crew! First, make sure you learn the steps about what to do before, during, and after each disaster. Then you will know the answers to the games. There is also a quiz at the end. By that time, you will be an expert on preparing for disaster!

By creating a disaster plan, making a disaster supplies kit, and working through this book, you will know what to do if a disaster ever strikes where you live. You and your family will be prepared. Being prepared is being ready!

After you complete the games in this book, there are ways for you to learn even more. Check out the Learn More section in the back of the book. Contact your local American Red Cross chapter. Learn about the emergency disaster plan in your community. Most of all, share what you learn with your family and friends.

Have fun! Ready...set ...prepare!

DISASTER CREW

RISING WATERS   "QUAKE" JOHNSON   BLAZE MARTINEZ   TOMMY TWISTER   STORMY KNIGHT   JOHNNY HURRICANE   SNOWY SINGH

TABLE OF CONTENTS

WORDS TO KNOW

Some words about disasters may be new to you. What are these words? What do they mean? Bright Shinely made a list of words to help you learn about disasters.

Aftershock: An aftershock is a small earthquake that often comes after a big earthquake.

Authorities: They are people who are in charge of a place during a disaster. They keep people safe. They can be police, or firefighters, or teachers.

Dangerous: Something is dangerous when it might hurt a person or destroy something. Playing with matches is dangerous.

Disaster: A disaster is a something that causes lots of damage to people and places. It can be a hurricane or a tornado. It can be a storm or a flood. It can be a fire, or an earthquake, or a blizzard.

Emergency: An emergency is something you do not expect. It is a time when someone could be in danger or could be hurt. It is a time to get help right away.

Evacuate: To evacuate means to leave a place in a quick and organized way. We sometimes evacuate during an emergency. When there is a fire drill at your school, you evacuate the school.

Hypothermia: This is a dangerous illness that can happen if your body gets much colder than normal. Hypothermia can happen if you spend a long time in a very cold place.

Magnitude: The magnitude of an earthquake tells us how much power the earthquake has. A high number like 7.0 means the earthquake is strong. A low number means the earthquake is weak.

Officials: These people hold important jobs in your area. They help carry out the rules we live by.

Plan: A plan is what to do next. A plan can list things to do in an emergency. Or it can be a picture of where things are. A disaster plan has the steps of what to do in all kinds of disasters. A fire escape plan can be a picture of your home that shows you how to get out in case of a fire.

Prepare: Getting prepared means getting ready. Getting prepared for a disaster means you will know what to do and where to go when a disaster happens.

Storm Surge: A storm surge is a large amount of water pushed on to shore by strong winds. A storm surge can be 50 to 100 miles wide. It can be 25 feet high. It can be as high as a two-story home!

Warning: A warning is issued by the National Weather Service over the radio and TV. A warning lets you know that bad weather has been seen where you live or is coming soon. When bad weather is close to your home, you need to take cover or evacuate right away so you can stay safe. Warnings can be about floods, thunderstorms, tornadoes, and hurricanes. A weather warning is more serious than a weather watch.

Watch: A watch is issued by the National Weather Service when bad weather might happen where you live. Watches are issued for floods, thunderstorms, tornadoes, and hurricanes. If they tell you there is a flood watch, it means that a flood might come. Your family needs to be prepared to move to higher ground. Listen to the radio or TV when there is watch so you will know what to do.

PREPARING FOR DISASTER

What does it mean to prepare for a disaster? It means that you find out all you can about disasters. Then you get ready for them.

Being prepared for a disaster is everyone's job. You can take steps to be prepared at home and at school. The first step is to learn about disasters and to make a disaster plan. Here are some ideas to help you get started!

Find out about disasters.

It is important to know about the kinds of disasters that can happen where you live and where you go to school. The best way to learn more is to ask questions.

With an adult, call your local emergency management office or local American Red Cross chapter. You can ask questions like these:

- What kinds of disasters can happen here?
- What can we do to be ready?
- How does our town warn us that a disaster is coming?
- How will I know what to do?
- How will we know when to evacuate?

Ask teachers and principals about the emergency plans at your school or care center.

Look at the Learn More section in the back of this book. You will see web sites to visit. You will see books to read. They can help you get even more prepared.

BE SURE THAT ALL FAMILY MEMBERS KNOW WHEN AND HOW TO DIAL 9-1-1

Make a plan.

Meet with your whole family to talk about your disaster plan. Be sure to tell them what you have learned about disasters. Tell them how important it is to be prepared! Your family can also meet with your caregivers. Start with these steps to make your family disaster plan.

- **Choose an out-of-town contact.** Ask your parents to choose someone to call in an emergency. This person will be your contact. It is best if your contact lives in a different town. Learn your contact's phone number by heart. Practice dialing it. Know when to call. A disaster might happen when you are not with your family. Then you can call your contact. Tell your contact where you are so your family can find you right away.

- **Decide where to meet with your family.** A disaster can happen when you are not with all of your family,

  o In case of a sudden emergency, like a fire, choose a place right outside your home.
  o In case you cannot go home, choose a meeting place outside your neighborhood.

- **Complete a Family Communications Plan.** How will you contact your family? How will you reach your out-of-town contact? Where will you meet? What are the emergency phone numbers? Post your family communications plan near the phone in your home. Ask your family to make copies of your plan. Each family member can carry it in a wallet or purse.

- **Plan for your pets.** If you evacuate, take your pets with you. Pets are not allowed in emergency shelters for health reasons.

UPDATE YOUR PLAN AT LEAST ONCE A YEAR!

4

YOUR FAMILY COMMUNICATIONS PLAN

If you have a family communications plan, it will be easy to contact your family or friends in a disaster! Fill out this emergency contact form with your family. Make sure they know where to meet and who to call. When you finish, cut out this page and hang it where all in your family can see it.

MY FAMILY COMMUNICATIONS PLAN

My Name: _____

My Address: _____

My Telephone Number: _____

My Family
Family work and cell numbers:

Work Number: _____

Cell Number: _____

Who to call in case of Emergency

Emergency Number:

9-1-1 or _____

Name and number of neighbor or relative:

_____

Name and number of out-of-town contact:

_____

5

MY FAMILY COMMUNICATIONS PLAN

More emergency numbers:

Local police station: _____

Local fire department: _____

Poison control: ___1-800-222-1222_____

Hospital emergency room: _____

Doctor: _____

Dentist: _____

Pharmacy: _____

Other important numbers:

_____   _____

_____   _____

_____   _____

TAKING CARE OF PETS

Do you have a pet? If you do, think about your pets in your disaster plans. If a disaster strikes, take your pets with you. If you have to evacuate, what are some things that a pet will need?

How much food should you take? What kind? _____

Circle other special items you will need:

Tank   Cage   Leash   Collar   Pet Carrier   Medicine   Toys/Chews

ID Tag Numbers: _____

Shot Types and Dates: _____

Emergency Contact Information for Pets

Pet Doctor (Vet)

Name: _____

Address: _____

Phone Number: _____

Kennel

Name: _____

Address: _____

Phone Number: _____

Pet-Loving Friend

Name: _____

Address: _____

Phone Number: _____

Nearest Hotel for Guests with Pets

Name: _____

Address: _____

Phone Number: _____

MAKING A DISASTER SUPPLIES KIT

During a disaster, you may have to evacuate quickly. You might not have time to gather all the supplies you need. That is why it is important to make a disaster supplies kit.

Remember to pack enough food, water, and supplies to last for three days for each person in your family. Place the supplies into a duffel bag or a backpack, Ask your parents to keep kits at home, at work, and in their cars.

Below is a list of sample list of items you need to have in your kit!
• Canned or dried foods that won't spoil
• Can opener that turns by hand
• Water (one gallon for each person each day)
• Flashlight
• Radio
• Extra batteries for the flashlight and radio
• First aid kit and handbook
• Soap, toilet paper, toothbrush, and other items to keep you clean
• Extra clothing and blankets
• Forks, spoons, knives, and paper plates
• Eye glasses and medicine
• Whistle
• Copies of IDs and credit cards
• Cash and coins
• A map of the area
• Baby food, bottles, and diapers
• Pet food if you have a pet

If you live in a cold area, you and your family have to think about staying warm! Include these other items in your kit:
• Jackets and coats
• Long pants and long sleeve shirts
• Sturdy shoes or boots
• Hats, mittens, and scarves
• Sleeping bags and warm blankets

Remember to update your disaster supplies kit at least once a year!

PLANNING YOUR OWN DISASTER SUPPLIES KIT

The Disaster Crew made kits for each of their families. Now you can make a kit for your own family by completing the worksheet below.

1. How many people are in your family? _____

2. Water: You need a 3-day supply. Each person needs 1 gallon per day. How many gallons will your family need?

   _____ people X 3 = _____ gallons of water.

3. Food: You need a 3-day supply of canned foods. List some foods you might put in your supplies kit:

   _____

   _____

4. Medicine and Supplies for your First Aid kit:

   _____

   _____

5. How will you listen to the news for weather updates and official instructions?

   _____

6. If the power goes out, what will you use to see in the dark?

   _____

7. What will you need to open cans of food?

   _____

PREVENT FIRES & BE SAFE

Fires spread quickly. If a fire breaks out in your home, there is no time. You have no time to pack the toys you love. You have no time to make phone calls. Heat and smoke from fire can be more dangerous than the flames. Breathing the super-hot air can hurt your lungs. If a fire starts, you need to get out of the home right away. Remember that firefighters will come to help you.

Prevent Fires

- If you find matches or a lighter, leave them alone. Go get an adult. Show the adult where you found the matches or lighter. Let the adult put them away.
- If you see a candle burning when no one else is in the room, do not touch it. Find an adult to blow out the candle.
- Keep objects like paper towels and pot holders away from the stove.

Be Safe

Smoke Alarms

- Do you have a smoke alarm on every floor of your home? Is one near the rooms where you sleep? Do you have enough smoke alarms where you live? If not, talk to your family. Ask an adult to install more smoke alarms.
- Remind an adult to test your smoke alarms once a month. Testing smoke alarms will help you know they are working. You will also know what they sound like.
- Your birthday comes once a year. Help your family change the smoke alarm batteries at least once a year, too. Help clean smoke alarms once a month.

Escape Safely

- Walk around in your home to all of the rooms. In each room, find at least TWO escape routes.
- Practice your fire escape plan at least two times every year.
- Practice meeting your family members at your outside meeting place.
- If a fire starts:
  - Get out and stay out.
  - Use your safest escape route – the one away from fire and smoke.
  - If you see a closed door, stop. Do not open it. Feel the door with the back of your hand. If the door is hot, leave it closed. Use a different way out. If the door is not hot, you can open it.
  - Crawl on your hands and knees. Crawl low under smoke. But keep your head up.
  - Meet at your outside meeting place.
  - Tell a family member to go to a friend's home and call 9-1-1.
  - Stay outside. It is only safe to go back inside after the firefighters say it is OK.

DID YOU KNOW... THAT MANY FIRES START OUT SMALL BUT GROW VERY QUICKLY? IF A FIRE STARTS, GET OUT FAST. STAY OUT. CALL 9-1-1 FROM A NEIGHBOR'S HOME.

BE SAFE! GET OUT!

What's up? I'm Blaze Martinez, the fire safety expert on the Disaster Crew. My job is to help you keep your cool during a fire emergency. If a fire starts, you can get out fast when you know two ways out of every room in your home. If one way is blocked by smoke or fire, use your second way out.

Draw a picture of three rooms in your home in the grids below. Make it show all the windows, doors and furniture. Then draw arrows that point to two safe ways out of each room.

Nice work! With your family, find two ways out of all other rooms in your home.

FLOODS

Floods are one of the most common disasters. They can be small – just in your neighborhood. They can be large – in many states at the same time.

All floods are not alike. Some floods grow slowly. They can grow over many days. Others floods grow quickly. They can happen in just a few minutes, even when it is not raining!

You need to know what to do when a flood occurs no matter where you live. Knowing what to do is even more important if you live in a low-lying place, or near water, or near a dam.

Before a Flood
- Learn about the chance of flooding in the places where you live and go to school.
- Know the ways to evacuate from your home and school. Practice these routes.

During a Flood

- Listen to the radio for news and official orders.
- If officials say to evacuate, you may have time. Make sure your home is safe. Ask your parents to bring in outdoor chairs and tables. Ask them to move important items to an upper floor. They need to unplug appliances, and turn off power at the main switches.
- Be aware that flash flooding can occur. If there is a flash flood, move to higher ground right away. Move no matter where you are.
- Turn around – do not drown. Never walk into floodwater. Remind your family to never drive into floodwater.

After a Flood
- Stay away from floodwater. It is very dirty.
- Return home only after authorities say it is safe.
- Throw away any food that touched floodwater. Help your family clean and remove germs from wet items.

WATER, WATER EVERYWHERE

Hi everyone, my name is Rising Waters. We all know that "April showers bring May flowers," but showers that turn into heavy rains can also cause floods. I'm here to remind you that during a flood, you and your family can get to higher ground to stay safe.

My friend Sasha needs your help! Last week, there was a lot of rain where she lives. Now the river in her town is rising fast. The river is spilling over its banks. There is flooding near her home. Help Sasha find her route to evacuate. Draw a path through the maze below. Help Sasha and her family get to a safe place!

THUNDERSTORMS

All thunderstorms are dangerous. Every thunderstorm has lightning. Strong thunderstorms can also bring heavy rains, high winds, hail, and tornadoes.

The sound of thunder can be very scary. Here are some tips on what to expect. Here is how to stay safe during a thunderstorm.

Before a Thunderstorm
- Learn the signs of a thunderstorm: dark clouds, lightning, and thunder.
- If you know a thunderstorm is coming, stay indoors. Pick something you can play inside.
- Learn the 30/30 rule to keep safe. If you see lightning, start counting to 30. If you hear thunder before you get to 30, go inside. Stay indoors for 30 minutes after the thunder has ended.

During a Thunderstorm
- If you are outside when a storm comes, go inside right away. A car is also a safe place.
- Crouch down, place your hands on your knees, and put your head down.
- Move away from things that lightning can strike. Stay away from trees, fences, phone lines, and power lines. Stay away from things made of metal.
- If you are in the water – such as a swimming pool or lake – get out of the water right away and go inside.
- If you are inside your home, tell your parents to unplug things like stoves, toasters, TVs, and phones.

After a Thunderstorm
- Wait indoors at least 30 minutes after the storm ends. Then it will be safe to go outside.

Hey, this is Stormy Knight! I am the Disaster Crew's safety expert on thunderstorms. I am here to show you how you can make your own lightning timer, quick as a flash. But first, do you know the 30-30 Rule for Lightning Safety? Here it is:

- 30 seconds or less from flash to bang, seek safety.

- 30 minutes after the last flash/bang, go back outside and play.

Make your own lightning timer! Choose two different colored crayons or markers. When the last flash or bang happens, draw arrows on the clock to show what time it is. Then add 30 minutes to that time. Draw another set of arrows using the other color. You will know how long to wait until you go outside.

TORNADOES

Tornadoes can happen all over the United States. Sometimes they happen quickly. There may be little or no warning.

Tornadoes have lots of power and can move fast. They are shaped like cones. They can strike the ground with winds up to 200 miles per hour. That is about four times faster than a car! Since tornadoes have so much power and can move very fast, you need to know what to do if a tornado strikes.

Before a Tornado
- Find a safe place in your home where you could go during a tornado. It could be in the basement. It could be in a small room with no windows. The room needs to be on the lowest floor.
- Learn the signs of a tornado: a dark, greenish sky; large hail; dark, low clouds; and loud roaring sounds.

During a Tornado
- Go to the safe place in your home. Make sure you stay away from the windows. If you have time, take your disaster supplies kit.
- If you are in a car, get out right away. Get inside a sturdy building.
- If you are outside and cannot get inside, go to a low ditch. Lie down. Cover your head with your hands.
- If you are in a mobile home or trailer, evacuate to a sturdy building. Most mobile homes and trailers provide no safety, even if tied down.

After a Tornado
- Stay away from any damage you see. Be sure to stay far away from damaged buildings or homes.
- Listen to the radio or TV. You will hear news and advice.

TORNADO WARNING SCRAMBLE

What's up, guys and girls? I'm Tommy Twister, the tornado safety expert. My job is to remind you to take action when there is a tornado warning in your area. To help you remember what to do before a tornado, I created a fun game for you with a twist – check it out!

Below is a list of words for you to unscramble. These are words that might come to mind when you think about tornadoes. First, unscramble each word. Then, look for the circled letter in each word. Copy these letters, in order, into the blank spaces near the bottom of the page. You will see a secret message!

arido __ __ __ (__)

wheater __ __ __ (__) __ __ __

ydwni __ __ __ (__) __

duclo __ (__) __ __ __

risbed __ __ __ (__) __ __

dorantoes __ __ __ __ __ __ __ __ (__)

nelfun (__) __ __ __ __ __

owl (__) __ __

doculy (__) __ __ __ __ __

terswit __ __ __ (__) __ __ __

G_ _O __U_ _A_E P_A__

Congratulations! Now you know what to do if there is a tornado warning!

17

HURRICANES

A hurricane is a type of tropical storm that has thunderstorms and strong winds. Hurricanes travel quickly across ocean waters. They cause serious damage to coastlines and nearby places.

A hurricane comes from the ocean. When it gets closer to land, it often brings heavy rains. It also brings strong winds and very high tides (storm surges). Hurricanes can also cause flooding and tornadoes.

Hurricanes travel a long way across the ocean. People have plenty of warning before hurricanes hit land. People have enough time to evacuate to a safe place and stay out of the storm's way. Learn what you can do to be safe if a hurricane comes.

Before a Hurricane
• Learn the way to evacuate with your family.
• Talk about what you would do when you evacuate. Discuss where you would go. Update your disaster supplies kit.
• Remind your parents to bring inside any items that can blow away during a hurricane.

During a Hurricane
• Stay indoors.
• Stay away from water and the shoreline.
• Evacuate if authorities say to do so. Keep in mind that heavy rains could cause roads to flood.
• Take your disaster supplies kit with you when you evacuate.
• Listen to the radio or TV for news.

After a Hurricane
• Return home only after authorities have told you to do so.

DID YOU KNOW... THAT TAPING WINDOWS DOES NOT STOP THEM FROM BREAKING DURING A HURRICANE? INSTEAD, YOU CAN DO JOBS THAT HELP YOU STAY SAFE. FOR EXAMPLE, MAKE SURE YOUR DISASTER SUPPLIES KIT IS READY.

DISASTER SUPPLIES KIT

HURRICANE HINTS

Dude, this is Johnny Hurricane and – you guessed it – I'm the Disaster Crew's hurricane safety expert. It is my job to remind you that if a hurricane ever heads toward your town, it is cool to be well prepared.

Complete the crossword puzzle below. When you do, you will find some awesome hints on what to do before, during, and after a hurricane.

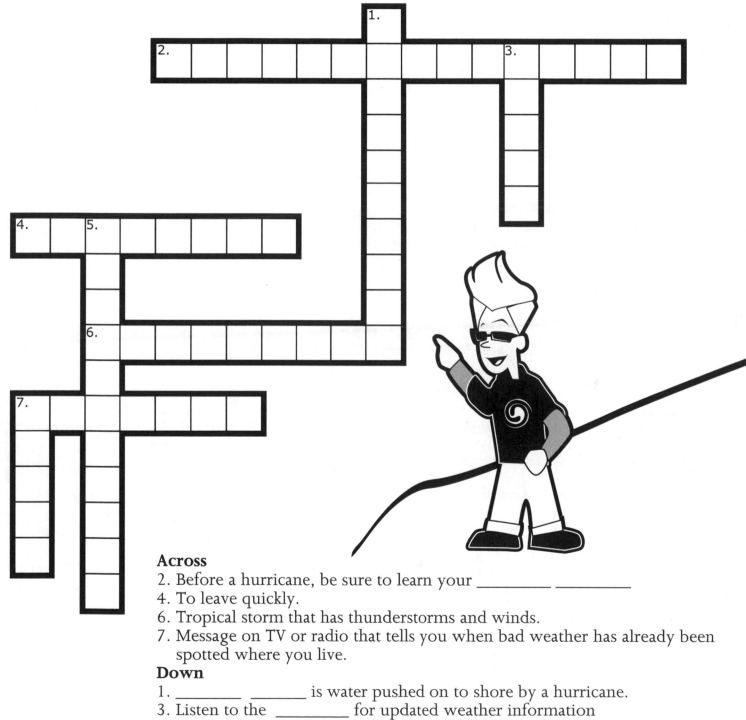

Across

2. Before a hurricane, be sure to learn your _____ _____
4. To leave quickly.
6. Tropical storm that has thunderstorms and winds.
7. Message on TV or radio that tells you when bad weather has already been spotted where you live.

Down

1. _____ _____ is water pushed on to shore by a hurricane.
3. Listen to the _____ for updated weather information
5. People who are in charge of a place or community.
7. Message on TV or radio that tells you about bad weather that might occur.

WINTER STORMS

Many places in the United States get winter storms every year. Even places that often have mild winters can be surprised by a winter storm! Winter storms can bring heavy snowfall and lots of ice. Winter storms can bring very cold air. Learn how to be safe during a winter storm.

Before a Winter Storm
- Add winter items to your disaster supplies kit: blankets, boots, hats, and mittens.
- Help your parents prepare a car safety kit. Include a bag of sand or kitty litter. Pack a shovel, snow brushes, window scrapers, and blankets.

During a Winter Storm
- If you must play or work in the snow, wear layers of warm clothing.
- Go inside often to get warm. Change your clothes if they are wet.
- If you start to shiver a lot, go inside right away. Go inside fast if you get very tired or turn very pale. Go inside fast if you get numb fingers, or toes, or ear lobes, or nose. You are getting too cold! These could be signs of illness (frostbite or hypothermia) due to the cold.
- Stay home unless you must travel.
- Listen to the radio or TV for weather reports and emergency news.

After a Winter Storm
- The air is still very cold and the wind can blow snow through the air. Dress warmly.
- Sidewalks and streets can be icy and very slippery. When snow blows, it can be hard to see where you are going. Be careful outdoors.

DID YOU KNOW... THAT IF YOU ARE STUCK IN THE CAR IN A SNOWSTORM, THE BEST THING TO DO IS STAY IN YOUR CAR? WAIT FOR HELP. DURING HEAVY SNOWSTORMS, PEOPLE WHO LEAVE THEIR CARS CAN GET LOST.

Hey there, this is Snowy Singh! It's a ball to play in the snow, and when you do, be sure to bundle up. As a winter storm safety expert, I can tell you that hats and mittens are a good start. It is also important to wear warm clothing in layers when you go outdoors. Wearing layers of clothing helps to keep you warm and dry.

In this word find game, circle all the winter clothes you can find. A list of words to look for is below.

```
L R F B K K K Z J S H P T X G
U E R Z C J A C K E T H Q A B
S T A S E Z I C S R E Y A L D
N A C N N P O E A R M U F F S
O E S F E S Q V M Y I U O G G
W W W B L Y A A L V R L O T L
S S L O T E L S N E T T I M O
U P O O R S E H Z W C W N M V
I W Z T U N A C P A R K A D E
T C U S T T H L E Q F G A M S
```

BOOTS	EARMUFFS	FLEECE
GLOVES	HAT	JACKET
LAYERS	MITTENS	PARKA
SCARF	SNOWSUIT	SWEATER
THERMALS	TURTLENECK	WOOL SOCKS

EARTHQUAKES

An earthquake is the sudden movement of the surface of the Earth. During an earthquake, you may notice a gentle shaking of the ground beneath your feet. You may notice objects wobbling on shelves. You may see hanging plants swaying back and forth. We cannot predict earthquakes – but scientists are working on it!

Earthquakes can be felt over large areas. They often last less than one minute. But, in that short time, they can do lots of damage. If the earthquake occurs in a big city, it may cause many deaths. It may hurt many people. Knowing what to do during an earthquake will help you be safe during this disaster.

Before an Earthquake
- In each room, find a safe place under a sturdy table, desk, or bench. Your safe place can also be against an inside wall or corner, away from things that could fall on you.
- Ask your parents to bolt or strap large items against the wall. Bolt to the walls mirrors, pictures, and tall bookcases. Keep heavy objects on the lower shelves so they do not fall on people.

During an Earthquake
- Drop, cover and hold on.
    - Take cover under a sturdy desk, table, or bench. Cover your face and head with your arms. Hold on.
    - If there is no table or desk near you, take cover along an inside wall or corner of the building. Cover your face and head with your arms. Hold on.
- Stay away from glass, windows, outside doors, and walls. Stay away from things that could fall.
- Stay inside until the shaking stops. Stay inside until it is safe to go outside.
- If you are outside, stay away from buildings, streetlights, and power poles.

After an Earthquake
- Be prepared for aftershocks.
- Open cabinets slowly. Beware of objects that can fall off shelves.
- Stay away from damaged places.

DID YOU KNOW... THAT DURING AN EARTHQUAKE, THE EARTH DOES NOT CRACK OPEN LIKE THE GRAND CANYON? INSTEAD, USUALLY THE EARTH'S SOIL SHIFTS UP AND DOWN AS THE EARTH RUMBLES AND MOVES.

HANDLE WITH CARE

What's up, gang? My friends in the Disaster Crew call me "Quake" Johnson. When I think about earthquakes, I try to think of ways to make the places around me safer. Then I tell my friends about them so they can stay safe too.

Below is a picture of my room. Can you help me find the things that might be dangerous in an earthquake? Use a blue crayon or pencil to draw a circle around the items that I can move so they will not fall on me. Use a red crayon or pencil to circle the items that an adult needs to move or fasten so they will not fall.

QUIZ!

ARE YOU PREPARED?

DISASTER SUPPLIES KIT

Now that you have completed the activities, let's see how prepared you are! Answer the questions below.

QUESTION 1. List five things you need to have in your disaster supplies kit.

QUESTION 2. Write the name and telephone number of your out-of-town contact.

QUESTION 3. List your two family meeting places.

QUESTION 4. During a fire, how do you check to see if a door is warm?

QUESTION 5. TRUE or FALSE? A Flash Flood Warning means that flooding has already been reported in your area.

QUESTION 6. If you cannot get inside during a thunderstorm, what do you need to do?

QUESTION 7. List three signs of a tornado.

QUESTION 8. TRUE or FALSE? Stay away from water and the shoreline during a hurricane.

QUESTION 9. What is a Winter Storm Warning?

QUESTION 10. Write one thing you need to do before an earthquake.

CERTIFICATE OF COMPLETION

Congratulations! By completing the activities in this book, you have demonstrated that you know how to prepare for all kinds of disasters. Great job!

Cut out this certificate and keep it where all in your family can see it.

READY...SET...PREPARED!

_____

(your name)

IS PREPARED FOR ALL DISASTERS!

I have learned how to work with my family to prepare for disasters. I can take action and make a difference by helping to:

✔ Create and post a family communications plan.

✔ Make a disaster supplies kit.

✔ Learn more about the kinds of disasters that could happen in my neighborhood.

✔ Select 2 family meeting places.

✔ Stay calm if a disaster strikes.

✔ Tell others about the dangers of fires, floods, thunderstorms, tornadoes, hurricanes, winter storms, and earthquakes.

Making a Disaster Supplies Kit
– page 9

Question 3: Answers may include: canned tuna, soup, beans, fruit, and vegetables

Question 4: Answers may include: bandages, aspirin, germ-free alcohol pads, antibiotic cream, sunscreen, thermometer, burn cream, medicine, band aids

Question 5: Radio that runs on batteries

Question 7: Can opener that turns by hand

Water, Water Everywhere
– page 13

ANSWER KEY

Lightning Timer
- page 15

Tornado Warning Scramble
– page 17

radi**o**
wea**t**her
wind**y**
cl**o**ud
deb**r**is
tornadoe**s**
funnel
low
cloudy
twist**e**r

The secret message is: **G O   T O   Y O U R   S A F E   P L A C E**

Hurricane Hazard Hint
— page 19

1. storm surge
2. evacuation route
3. radio
4. evacuate
5. authorities
6. hurricane
7. warning / watch

Bundle Up!
— page 21

BOOTS   EARMUFFS   FLEECE
GLOVES   HAT   JACKET
LAYERS   MITTENS   PARKA
SCARF   SNOWSUIT   SWEATER
THERMALS   TURTLENECK   WOOL SOCKS

ANSWER KEY

Handle with Care
– page 23

Quiz
– page 25

Question 1:   Answers may include: canned or dried food, can opener, water, flashlight, batteries, radio, first aid kit, soap, toothbrush, clothes, forks, spoons, knives, medicine, whistle, map, money, baby food, pet food

Question 4:   Feel the door with the back of your hand.

Question 5:   True

Question 6:   Hurry to a low, open space right away. Crouch down, place your hands on your knees, and put your head down.

Question 7:   Answers may include: a dark, greenish sky; large hail; low clouds; loud roaring sounds

Question 8:   True

Question 9:   A Winter Storm Warning lets you know that bad weather has been seen where you live or is coming soon.

Question 10: Answers may include:
• In each room in your home, find a safe place under a sturdy desk, table, or bench.
• Keep heavy objects on lower shelves so they do not fall on people.
• Ask your parents to bolt or strap large items against the wall so they will not fall.

Online Resources

Are You Ready? online:
www.fema.gov/areyouready

USFA for Kids:
www.usfa.fema.gov/kids

Citizen Corps:
www.citizencorps.gov

FEMA for Kids:
www.fema.gov/kids

FEMA Hazard Maps:
www.hazardmaps.gov

American Red Cross:
www.redcross.org

Ready Campaign:
www.ready.gov

National Weather Service:
www.nws.noaa.gov

American Red Cross - Masters of Disaster®
www.redcross.org/disaster/masters

U.S. Geological Survey
www.usgs.gov

Print Resources

Are You Ready? An In-depth Guide to Citizen Preparedness (IS-22)

Preparing for Disaster (FEMA 475) (A4600) Also available in Spanish.

Preparing for Disaster for People with Disabilities and other Special Needs (FEMA 476) (A4497) Also available in Spanish.

Food and Water in an Emergency (FEMA 477) (A5055) Also available in Spanish.

Helping Children Cope with Disaster (FEMA 478) (A4499) Also available in Spanish.

The Adventures of Julia and Robbie -- The Disaster Twins (Storybook) (FEMA 344)

Ready...Set...Prepare! For Ages 4-7 (FEMA 522) (A2210)

To request additional FEMA publications, call the FEMA Distribution Center at (800) 480-2520 or write to:

Federal Emergency Management Agency
P.O. Box 2012
Jessup, MD 20794-2012

To request additional American Red Cross publications, contact your local Red Cross chapter. Find your local chapter by typing in your ZIP Code at www.redcross.org.

This activity book is offered to you by Federal Emergency Management Agency's Community and Family Preparedness Program and American Red Cross Community Disaster Education. These programs are nationwide efforts to help people prepare for disasters of all types.